Precolumbian
Terracottas

Precolumbian Terracottas

Franco Monti

Paul Hamlyn

LONDON · NEW YORK · SYDNEY · TORONTO

Translated by Margaret Crosland from the Italian original
Terrecotte Precolombiane
© *1966 Fratelli Fabbri Editori, Milan*
This edition © *1969*
THE HAMLYN PUBLISHING GROUP LIMITED
LONDON · NEW YORK · SYDNEY · TORONTO
Hamlyn House, Feltham, Middlesex, England
Text filmset in Great Britain by
Yendall & Co. Ltd., London
Printed in Italy by
Fratelli Fabbri Editori, Milan

INTRODUCTION

It is still impossible to determine with any exactitude when terracotta first appeared on the American continent; nor is there any proof of whether it was a native invention or a later introduction following migrationary movements. According to some experts it evolved in the following way: receptacles woven from twigs and then covered with a layer of clay to strengthen them were accidentally placed near a fire, and so became hard and waterproof. This led to baskets being covered with clay and baked on purpose, and finally to the creation of shapes without the support of twigs.

Earthenware vessels are regarded as a typical product of agricultural peoples: they can be used to cook food, to contain water for an unlimited period and to preserve and protect provisions, especially grain, from rodents. On the other hand, they are not so useful in nomadic communities who hunt and live on berries and wild fruit, for they are heavy and liable to break when moved, unlike receptacles made from bark, twigs or wood. Moreover, archaeological research confirms that sites where ancient terracottas have been found had previously been inhabited by societies with an agricultural economy.

Terracotta did not however acquire the same importance or reach the same aesthetic standard over the whole of the American continent. And here we shall not be considering any of the areas—such as the United States—where discoveries are more interesting from the archaeological than from the artistic point of view, or where they are not the typical expression of an indigenous culture, or where, as on the east coast of the South American Andes, their artistic interest is limited and so far unassessed.

Some earthenware is simple, even rough, in shape, for it was destined for purely practical use. Other work, intended for religious and ritualistic purposes, is more ambitious and less utilitarian, and reveals a genuine ambition to create objects that were also aesthetically satisfying. It is difficult, however, to establish a scale of artistic values related to a chronological order since (as has often been pointed out) the forms, decoration and colours of the earliest ceramics are as developed and refined as those of later work.

The term terracotta is generally used to describe all types of baked clay, though it is also applied more specifically to a type of somewhat raw clay, which after firing assumes a colour varying from yellow ochre to red and is not varnished; Precolumbian terracotta is usually of this type. (The term Precolumbian, which is used to describe the ancient cultures of the American continent, should not be used only in its narrow sense of 'before the arrival of Christopher Columbus' but rather to describe that long period lasting from the origin of local cultures to the date at which they came under obvious European influence.) Once the clay has been dug out, it is usually left standing for some time before being used. Highly plastic and naturally waterproof clays, although more malleable, are extremely liable to shrink and crack during drying and firing; for this reason they have to be mixed with non-plastic substances such as sand, mica, carbon compounds—waxes, dried dung—finely crushed rock and shells, or small fragments of terracotta.

Extremely detailed knowledge was therefore needed on the following points: where the right clay could be found; with what ingredients and in what proportions it should be mixed; how long it should rest; how much it should be worked; what type of heat should be used for firing it; how long the firing should last and how it should be regulated. The skill of the craftsman depended on a correct assessment of all these elements. According to European historians, the Old World was the first to adopt the wheel for the manufacture of earthenware—a form of mechanisation compared to the previous use of the hands alone. Yet the wheel was unknown in the American continent—an astonishing fact when one considers the perfect symmetry of the forms and the identical thickness of the sides.

There were three methods in general use. In the first of these, a compact block of clay was gradually hollowed out inside until the sides reached the necessary thinness. The base and the neck were usually

1. Seated figure, of the type described as 'baby face'.
Height 14½ in. Tlatilco, State of Mexico, Private collection,
Mexico City.

2. Vase in the shape of a duck. Height $8\frac{1}{4}$ in. Tlatilco,
State of Mexico. Museo Nacional de Antropología,
Mexico City.

3. Small female figure. Height 6½ in. Tlatilco. State of Mexico. Private collection, Milan.

1.   Seated figure, of the type described as 'baby face'. Height 14½ in. Tlatilco, State of Mexico. Private collection, Mexico City. The significance of these unusual figures of child-like appearance is still obscure; they are extremely rare, and were probably connected with a traditional Olmec cult.

2.   Vase in the shape of a duck. Height 8¼ in. Tlatilco, State of Mexico. Museo Nacional de Antropología, Mexico City. This bird recurs frequently in Tlatilco pottery, which has a particular bias toward animal subjects.

3.   Small female figure. Height 6½ in. Tlatilco, State of Mexico. Private collection, Milan. Figures of this type have been found throughout the Valley of Mexico. Most of them are female, with obvious sexual characteristics: they are marked by a certain formal refinement and by the variety of their detail.

4.   Mask with large ear-discs. Height 4 ft. Teotihuacán, State of Mexico. Museo Nacional de Antropología, Mexico City. Terracotta masks are less frequent than stone ones but both have several stylistic features in common; a ritual significance is sometimes attributed to them.

5.   Tripod vase with fresco decoration. Height 3½ in. Teotihuacán, State of Mexico. Private collection, Milan. The brilliant and sophisticated decoration adorning this type of vase is painted on a layer of plaster applied to the terracotta after firing; the ornamentation, which is always very rich, consists of geometric and curvilinear motifs.

4.   Mask with large ear-discs. Height 4 ft. Teotihuacán, State of Mexico. Museo Nacional de Antropología, Mexico City.

5. Tripod vase with fresco decoration. Height $3\frac{1}{2}$ in.
Teotihuacán, State of Mexico. Private collection, Milan.

made separately and then carefully joined to the main part of the object; all trace of the join was then removed. A more widely used technique was the 'Colombian' method, in which the walls of the vessel were built up by winding a thread of clay round and round from the bottom to the top; finally, the outside was carefully smoothed and made uniform either by hand or with a spatula until there was no trace of the spirals except for slight ridges inside. Sometimes the two techniques were combined: a block of clay was used as a base from which to start the spirals.

The third technique, the use of moulds for making the entire object or only part of it, appears to have been general from the beginning of the history of ceramics, as is shown by the quantities found in Peru, Central America and Mexico; its products can be richly decorated with a light impasto and are less liable to crack during firing. To produce a mould a model was executed entirely in the round and then carefully covered with a layer of soft clay, applied so that it penetrated the hollowed-out parts and adhered to the raised ones; a vertical cross-section of this outer layer was then made, and the resulting two parts of the mould when filled in turn with clay and joined together again produced an object identical with the original. This was retouched and completed by hand with different details, so it is rare to find two completely identical objects in Precolumbian art. In vessels for example, the base and the handle were put on afterwards and often details in high relief were added before firing to objects modelled by hand. During the drying stage, many of the terracottas were either wholly or partly immersed in a bath of water and powdered clay, which closed the pores and made the object waterproof; this kind of slip was then polished to give a particular translucence to the finished work, and the painted decoration, made from vegetable and mineral pigments, superimposed on it. Some peoples paid great attention to the final smoothing down, which was carried out with pieces of leather, shells or chips of stone. As is well known, the colour of a ceramic depends either on the composition of the clay or on the method of firing. Of the components iron was the only colouring element; when it was heated the resulting oxidation produced a colour ranging from a light grey-blue tone to deep black, sometimes with metallic glints. For the firing process, therefore, fairly complex ovens had to be prepared, according to the nature of the impasto. It was simpler to use an open fire, but this could never achieve high temperatures and the smoke tended to give the earthenware a blackish colouring; in closed ovens, where it was possible to regulate the draught, higher temperatures could be used to produce different colours.

A form of oven that seems to have been widely used consisted of an opening hollowed out of the ground, in which the objects to be fired were placed and covered with highly combustible material. Sometimes a protective layer of terracotta potsherds was placed between the fire and the earthenware. Variations in temperature produced a colouring that was black, grey or a pronounced shade of red. Some objects could be given a particular brilliance by adding broken charcoal to the clay, which was then vigorously polished after firing.

One type of ceramic, described as 'plumbate', has near-metallic highlights that enhance the colouring with tones varying from grey to dark green and red-brown; it seems to have been proved now that this effect was achieved by using a slip rich in iron and aluminium, which became vitrified in a sufficiently high temperature.

An astonishing variety of forms and types can be found in Precolumbian ceramics, whose art often approaches real sculpture in its dimensions, its creative imagination and excellent technique. Pottery included domestic vessels and also others used only in religious or funeral ceremonies; these were often in the form of musical instruments or utensils, which were placed in a tomb with the corpse. Some types of pottery can be classed as fundamental because they recur in different styles in many cultures. It is possible, therefore, to classify objects both generally, on the basis of their form, and more specifically, according to their decoration. The tripod vessel, for example, which probably evolved for practical reasons since the three supporting feet gave more balance, is one of the earliest shapes and one that apparently existed all over Mexico and Central America. It is incredible to see the number and types of variations made possible by the three-legged design: the legs can be completely vertical or bend outwards or they can be hollow, with an open slit and containing a small ball in the shape of a bell. The vertical legs are usually strictly geometrical—cylindrical and parallel to one another—but those at an angle take many forms; an early example is a mammary form, which can also be completely rounded. There are feet that narrow to a point or that curve either inwards or outwards; others are carved in stylised versions of heads, skulls, caryatids, animals, or birds—a feature found in almost all the cultures of Central America.

Vessels in globular form or in the shape of simple cups, supported by feet of conical-trunk shape, are also fairly common, though in Mexico they appear only after the Toltec period. The great goblet—the *kero*—with a rounded base, which originated perhaps at Nazca in Peru, although not very widespread lasted for a long time, right up to the Inca period. (A flat-based version also appears in Tiahuanaco.) Nevertheless it was by no means completely unknown in other cultures, for example, in that of Chimu, where it was also made in gold and silver. More typical of the South American continent is the double vessel, in which the two globular sections are placed side by side—as often happens in Peru—or superimposed one on top of the other. In many examples only one of the two sections is provided with a spout; as the vessel is tilted, however, the liquid passes into it from the other communicating section through a whistle,

6.　Small female figure. Height 4 in. Chupícuaro, State of Guanajuato, Mexico. Museum of the American Indian, New York. This surprisingly delicate female figure, which still shows clear traces of the original polychrome decoration, represents the more primitive style of western Mexico; these figurines are believed by some to have been used for funerary purposes.

7.　Seated figure holding a dish. Height 19½ in. State of Jalisco, Mexico. Museum of Primitive Art, New York. This sculpture was discovered in Jalisco but a certain fullness of shape and such physical details as the size of the eyes are more characteristic of Colima work; this mingling of styles is not un- common in western Mexico.

8.　Seated female figure. Height 12 in. Etzatlan, State of Jalisco, Mexico. Private collection, Milan. This work, with its outstandingly refined modelling, is also remarkable for its ani- mation; the mobility of the face is matched by the restrained eloquence of the raised arms and the grace of the lower limbs.

6.　Small female figure. Height 4 in. Chupícuaro, State of Guanajuato, Mexico. Museum of the American Indian, New York.

7. Seated figure holding a dish. Height 19½ in. State of
Jalisco, Mexico. Museum of Primitive Art, New York.

8.   Seated female figure. Height 12 in. Etzatlan, State of
Jalisco, Mexico. Private collection, Milan.

which emits a slight sound perhaps intended to imitate, in funerary objects, the panting breath of a dying man. Sometimes certain forms and designs are repeated in a very similar way in different cultures; for example, some Peruvian Chimu vases are identical with a type common in Ecuador. (In Colombia, on the other hand, vessels with two sections superimposed on each other are more usual.) Funerary vessels with human or animal figures on them recur however in different and widely separated regions, presenting a very extensive range of styles; this is best exemplified by the vessels in the shape of human heads, with or without handles, belonging to the Mochica culture.

When trying to date or place forms that are fundamentally similar, it is always necessary to start by examining the details; handles, for instance, are particularly significant. For example the 'stirrup' handle, which is semicircular in shape and is set either vertically or at an oblique angle to the vase, is confined almost exclusively to the northern coast of Peru except for sporadic appearances in Mexico during the preclassical era. The handles are generally of two different kinds: they can be flattened and horizontal, forming a kind of bridge between the two parts of the double vessels with two figures, as in some examples from Peru—Nazca, Mochica and Chimu—and from Cauca in Colombia, while a flattened and arched form is found on single vessels. The second type comprises double handles placed symmetrically on the sides of the receptacle, which seem to have been introduced rather late; they are often placed between the head and tail of the bird-shaped Inca *aryballoi,* where they act more or less as holders.

As we have already pointed out, Precolumbian ceramics do not consist entirely of earthenware vessels. An outstanding and, from a sculptural point of view, more significant branch comprises statuettes and statues representing human figures, animals, or fantastic beings—deities or demons—with a variety of attributes. This type of figurative terracotta has provided ethnologists with an extremely important source of information on ancient cultures. The figures, like the earthenware vessels in figurative form, reveal physical characteristics, malformations and illnesses, and the various gestures and ornaments used by different peoples. They also supply evidence on clothing and adornment in relation to climate and different social strata; on everyday activities and their utensils, weapons and instruments; on attitudes to religion including evidence of specific ceremonies and cults. In short, they make it possible to build up an impression of the complexity and richness of a culture. They also supply remarkable documentary evidence about ancient architecture, both social and religious, on the flora and fauna and on the heavily populated religious pantheon.

Over the entire continent (with the exception of Peru), a great number of anthropomorphous statuettes have come to light. Standing about four inches high, with small heads, these are worked entirely in the round and all are clearly the products of various different styles. In the Maya region, on the other hand, statuettes reaching a height of eight inches have been found, while elsewhere, particularly in Mexico, human figures and animals are as high as three feet or, exceptionally, even more. It is not unusual to find sculpture representing houses complete with inhabitants, and also scenes from daily life—domestic activities, games, religious ceremonies—in which people and animals are fixed on to the same base. There is an abundance of utensils, spindles, perfume-burners, moulds for reproducing objects, for decorating earthenware and textiles or for tattooing. The tattoo instruments are of two kinds: a cylindrical type perforated inside that produced a continuous pattern or actual shapes, either rectangular or circular—sometimes appropriately designed to follow the line of the limbs. In addition, many musical instruments of various types can be found in almost all cultures: flutes, trumpets, ocarinas, whistles and bells.

A basic element, and one that is therefore indispensable to the classification of styles, is decoration. This always derives from three fundamental methods, subtraction, addition and moulds, which can be used either single or together. In the first of these, designs were incised and impressed on the clay while it was still wet with a piece of pointed bone or silex, or else a spatula. Alternatively, part of the surface was removed when the clay was either wet or dry or even after it had been fired, thus bringing into relief motifs

9. Barking dog. Height 7½ in. State of Colima, Mexico.
Museo Nacional de Antropología, Mexico City.

10. Prisoner in chains. Height 13½ in. State of Colima, Mexico. Private collection, Mexico City.

11. Copulating couple. Height 15½ in. State of Jalisco, Mexico. Private collection, Mexico City.

9.   Barking dog. Height $7\frac{1}{2}$ in. State of Colima, Mexico. Museo Nacional de Antropología, Mexico City. This breed of Mexican dog, which was hairless and reared as food, recurs frequently in Colima ceramics. Often modelled like a vase, it was portrayed in various attitudes and coloured red, sometimes with red-black markings, which create a good impression of the coat.

10.   Prisoner in chains. Height $13\frac{1}{2}$ in. State of Colima, Mexico. Private collection, Mexico City. The technique of modelling in soft lines and curves, which is characteristic of Colima art, is clearly illustrated by this expressive figure. The striking composure and calm facial expression harmonise with the fullness of the contours.

11.   Copulating couple. Height $15\frac{1}{2}$ in. State of Jalisco, Mexico. Private collection, Mexico City. Here expression is almost entirely concentrated in the elongated faces with their ecstatic, dilated eyes, large mouths and long pointed noses.

12.   Seated male figure. Height $27\frac{1}{2}$ in. Ixtlan del Rio, State of Nayarit, Mexico. Museo Antropológico de Guadalajara, Guadalajara. In this majestically posed figure, the face is set in the impassive severity of death, while the anatomy of the body is comparatively life-like.

13.   Warrior. Height $12\frac{1}{2}$ in. State of Colima, Mexico. Museo Nacional de Antropología, Mexico City. This figure belongs to the gallery of individual portraits that, by the diversity of their pose and clothing, illustrate the varied activities of life in this type of culture.

12. Seated male figure. Height 27½ in. Ixtlan del Rio, State
of Nayarit, Mexico. Museo Antropológico de Guadalajara,
Guadalajara.

13. Warrior. Height 12½ in. State of Colima, Mexico. Museo
Nacional de Antropología, Mexico City.

and figures already placed in position: this technique was used throughout the Maya and Teotihuacán cultures. Decoration was added by arranging on the object, while it was still wet, simple pats and fillets of clay, small heads, animal figures and so on, sometimes made from moulds.

There were numerous techniques for applying colour during various stages of the work either before or after firing, on wet or dry clay or on a layer of stucco on the clay in advance. In the most ancient method of painting, which was a kind of 'negative' process, the terracotta was given a colour bath after the decorative motifs incised by the artist had been covered by a layer of wax, which disappeared after firing. This technique was used in Peru and Mexico in the Ticomán, Teotihuacán and Maya cultures, as well as in the north-west. The sophisticated 'fresco' decoration used as a base a thin layer of stucco placed over the vessel after firing. (The same technique and colours—pink, yellow, azure and green—enrich the mural frescoes of Teotihuacán and Kaminaljuyú, in Guatemala.) Sometimes, however, details in relief are painted directly on the vessel, without any preparation of the clay base. Here the colour is not so durable, since it could not fuse with the clay during firing; as a result many objects have lost their original bright and multi-coloured decorations through the years and to-day appear misleadingly bare and simple. For example, many Maya figurines from the island of Jaina retain at best minute traces, often almost indecipherable, of their splendid colour range. Usually however colouring was added before firing; this varies, according to the stylistic evolution of the particular culture, from the simple geometric type of decoration used in the preclassical era to the later use of realistic motifs or the true representation of scenes with large numbers of people, often including hieroglyphic motifs. This system of colouring reached a generally high standard of competence during the classical era, though obviously some cultures developed individual stylistic characteristics of their own; among the Mochica of Peru, for instance, only two colours were used—a bright or brownish shade of red, and cream—while among the Nazca, decoration is always in a rich range of colours. It is interesting to note that, particularly in Central and South America, decoration in colour was often partly in relief on the same vessel, especially on human and animal figures, in which one part of the body stands out in relief while the other features are painted only. Particularly sophisticated effects are obtained by adding different layers of colour between one process of firing and the next; this is especially common in the famous Cholula vessels, of which unfortunately only a few rare examples have survived intact. Sometimes—as among the Maya—the two methods of adding and subtracting can be combined in the same work; special effects are obtained by adding clay parts in various colours to the places that had previously been hollowed out. A final type of ornamentation—which occurs often in the black vessels from Chimu and certain Maya and Aztec states—consists of ceramic moulds pressed on to the clay before it dried.

The styles produced by Precolumbian American cultures are so varied that it is impossible to generalise about them: each must be examined separately in its correct chronological context and in the light of its ethnic and historical development. The art forms of each culture and each region of the American continent are so individual that they can be accurately distinguished even from those of its nearest neighbours. Thus an expert in this field can almost always pinpoint the place of origin of a discovery by examining its style—for example, by the way in which the human figure is portrayed, or the detailing, or the emphasis put on particular characteristics or the type of decoration—all elements that derive from the traditional ritual or symbolism peculiar to each culture. Further, at a particular stage in its evolution, the art forms of a culture have certain well-defined characteristics. Thus the figurines of the preclassical era are immediately distinguishable, either by their physical features, exaggerated rotundity and extravagant sexual attributes—a lack of proportion that also characterises not only the well-known Paleolithic Venuses in Europe but also the great family of primitive sculpture left scattered all over the world during the prehistoric period—or by decoration based principally on the incision of lines and dots or on the application of pats and fillets of clay to express the features of the face and the details. The ingenuity of this art while still in its infancy is clear not only in the distortion of the limbs—a simple way of expressing symbols —but also in the rough technique that, while still searching for a complete means of expression, nevertheless succeeds in capturing and conveying a feeling of intense vitality.

In comparison, the art of the classical period seems derivative, although it is also characterised by a search for naturalism and by a deliberate synthetic quality. The latest period of all is marked by a striving for effect and a sophisticated quality in the decoration, which often develops into a rich and baroque style. But the fundamental quality of Precolumbian art is the great vitality and dynamic power that animate the extraordinarily plastic forms, thrown into relief by skilful colouring. Many examples can compare with advantage—and not only from the technical point of view—with the best work of the most important civilisations of the ancient world, such as those of Egypt and Greece. The term 'primitive', which in the past was sometimes applied to this art because of its alleged inability to represent reality, now appears misguided not only because our taste has been influenced by modern art but because of the numerous examples that have recently been discovered. The ancient American artist was certainly capable of representing objects realistically, but this was not his prime interest any more than it is that of the modern artist. It was not a question of copying nature, but rather of interpret-

14. Figure of a seated woman. Height 18½ in. State of Michoacán, Mexico. Museum of the American Indian, New York.

14.   Figure of a seated woman. Height 18½ in. State of Michoacán, Mexico. Museum of the American Indian, New York. A figure remarkable for harmonious composition and sensitive modelling; the bare simplicity of its construction throws into relief the details of the ornaments, the ear-rings, necklace and armlets. Although the polychrome decoration has almost completely disappeared, this does not affect the essential beauty of the image.

15.   Figure of a seated man. Height 13½ in. State of Nayarit, Mexico. Private collection, Milan. The figure holds a rattle in his right hand. In contrast to the more usual type of sculpture with grotesque features and varied, bright polychrome colouring, this example is distinguished by a certain harmony in the contours, the realistic expression of the face and the moderate colouring.

16.   Vase in the shape of a human head. Height 11 in. Zaachila, State of Oaxaca, Mexico. Museo Nacional de Antropología, Mexico City. Earthenware funerary objects in the Zapotec culture, though remarkable for the richness of their subject matter, all reflect the unusual stylistic traditions of the region. This is particularly true of centres such as Zaachila, to which this head belongs, during the last phase of the Monte Albán period.

17.   Urn representing a jaguar. Height 3 ft. Monte Albán, State of Oaxaca, Mexico. Museo Nacional de Antropología, Mexico City. The funerary urn—found in tombs, temples, or in niches over doors—is the most typical expression of Zapotec culture; usually it is in the form of a human figure with fairly complex decoration. This example is unusual both for its size and the use of the colour green, which is rare in ceramics.

15. Figure of a seated man. Height 13½ in. State of Nayarit, Mexico. Private collection, Milan.

16. Vase in the shape of a human head. Height 11 in. Zaachila, State of Oaxaca, Mexico. Museo Nacional de Antropología, Mexico City.

17. Urn representing a jaguar. Height 3 ft. Monte Albán, State of Oaxaca, Mexico. Museo Nacional de Antropología, Mexico City.

ing it according to his personal emotions and view of the world. Lastly, it must be emphasised that a clear feeling of monumentality lies behind this art, which suceeds in giving—even in works of reduced dimensions—such a life-like quality that they could be enlarged indefinitely without losing balance or proportions, delicacy of detail or expressive intensity.

Representations of men, gods, animals and objects are found alongside the production of earthenware vessels in almost all areas; but while they occupy a position of pre-eminence in the Mexican and Central American cultures, they are less important or even nonexistent in South America. Everywhere, art seems to be inspired by religion which, especially in the period of the great flowering of cultures, was the common denominator of all strata of society. To understand the religious symbolism that permeates all forms of art—a symbolism so complex that it is difficult to grasp its original meaning—it is necessary to search out, by means of the artist's work, those feelings common to mankind since its beginnings—that is, terror, a sense of mystery, a delight in beauty, joy in the power of the sun, and horror of darkness. Most objects have been found in tombs: protective gods, guides, companions or slaves for the journey towards the unknown, all of which testify to a belief in a life beyond and the existence of ritual links with death.

The chronological reconstruction of ancient American history has always been the principal aim of archaeologists. The study of geological strata, the first method to be adopted (and still considered today as the basic approach to this type of evaluation), has led to the first general classification of types and styles of materials; no dates however have been fixed by the analysis of texts and inscriptions. The radiocarbon method of dating, invented in 1947 by the American Libby, has already proved very valuable and will be even more so in the future. It is based on the rate of disintegration—produced by cosmic rays—of the amount of Carbon 14 existing in all organic substances. Since the speed of this process is more or less constant, the age of an object can be estimated reasonably accurately by measuring the amount of Carbon 14 remaining in it. However, only a few dates have so far been obtained with this method, though they have, even so, partly invalidated the old existing chronology, which at best is shaky and at worst almost non-existent. Nevertheless, there is still in use a subdivision according to which the history of the whole of the American continent is divided into three major cultural periods, preclassical, classical and post-classical. Preclassical is here understood to mean the pre-Christian era, during which the first forms of social life developed at the same time as the village. The classical period comprises the first millennium AD, which saw the rise and fall of the theocratic states, while the last period, which began towards the end of the second century, saw the rise of the feudal aristocracy on the crest of the wave of military expansion.

The high plateau of Mexico is perhaps the best-

18. Seated figure. Height 8 in. State of Oaxaca, Mexico.
Museo Nacional de Antropología, Mexico City.

19. Funerary urn. Height 1 ft 8 in. State of Oaxaca, Mexico.
Museum of the American Indian, New York.

20. Tripod vessel. Height 7½ in. Zaachila, State of Oaxaca, Mexico. Museo Nacional de Antropología, Mexico City.

18. Seated figure. Height 8 in. State of Oaxaca, Mexico. Museo Nacional de Antropología, Mexico City. This figure is chiefly remarkable for its simple shapes, geometrical composition and intense expression. Its ingenuous grace, together with the straightforward construction of the lines and volumes, place it in the initial phase of the Zapotec culture; the features and technique reveal an Olmec influence.

19. Funerary urn. Height 1 ft 8 in. State of Oaxaca, Mexico. Museum of the American Indian, New York. Urns in the shape of human figures are reasonably common in Zapotec art and were probably used either as votive offerings or as censers. These often fantastically detailed creations—usually representing gods—are built up partly from moulds and partly from modelled additions.

20. Tripod vessel. Height $7\frac{1}{2}$ in. Zaachila, State of Oaxaca, Mexico. Museo Nacional de Antropología, Mexico City. The beautiful polychrome decoration and the three supporting legs in the form of snakes are characteristic of the classical period in the Mixtec culture; this example, whose shape is somewhat unusual, comes from Zaachila.

21. Kneeling figure. Chalco, State of Mexico. Private collection, Los Angeles. This vessel belongs to a type of 'plumbate' ceramic, dating from the preclassical period, found over a vast area that includes western Mexico, Guatemala and San Salvador. This example, with its striking plaster relief, dates from shortly before the Aztec period, and can be attributed to the Mixtec culture.

21. Kneeling figure. Chalco, State of Mexico. Private
collection, Los Angeles.

known area archaeologically; it is also outstanding for the duration and continuity of its cultural history. From the centre of the Mexican region, an all-pervading artistic influence radiates over the United States—both to the south-east and the south-west—over the Maya regions and in fact as far as the western coasts of South America. The valley of Mexico, which intersects the plateau at altitudes varying from six to nine thousand feet, was the site (perhaps because of its particularly favourable climate) of the first settlements of the American agricultural population. There is much evidence of the varied cultural phases that succeeded one another in this area; during the pre-classical era the regions that are archaeologically the most important (because of the rich yields from the tombs and funerary remains) are Copilco, Zacatenco, El Arbolillo, Cuicuilco and Ticomán, centres that, in view of the depth of the stratification deposits, were certainly inhabited for many centuries. Finds consist of tripod vessels with feet, usually in a mammary form, and of large monochrome containers in white, black or dark brown decorated with simple geometric incisions carried out before firing; female figures also appear, most of them with fragmentary faces, their features made up from pats and fillets of clay added separately.

Later periods are marked by the appearance of conical globular and cylindrical vessels decorated in two colours, such as white on red or red on white, and of extremely varied figured vessels, often incised after firing with motifs representing gods in animal form: vessels with stirrup-type handles, which are widespread throughout Peruvian ceramics, are also found. These are succeeded by examples painted in red and white on a yellow background, often surrounded by incisions, and finally, a form of negative painting, or rather a fresco decoration on stucco applied after firing. The figurines—usually between four and six inches high, though in exceptional cases reaching 20 to 24 inches—are carved, and depict a variety of human types, some wearing a few clothes and others with misshapen skulls, tattoo marks and filed teeth. The human figures include dwarfs, dancers, acrobats, musicians, warriors, people playing ball games, all lively and realistic portraits. The most interesting examples, thought to belong to the Zacatenco culture, were found at Tlatilco, a region not far from Mexico City. They represent almost exclusively a type of young woman characterised by a slender torso, small breasts, short arms, hips and legs accentuated to an exaggerated extent, and tiny feet. With the exception of a few figures who wear short dresses, they are unclothed and adorned only with more or less elaborate jewellery; traces of red colouring are often also visible. Some very unusual figures have two heads; others have only one head but the outline of two faces can be seen superimposed one upon the other. Probably these terracottas were intended to represent an ideal concept of female beauty rather than a symbolic image linked with a religious ritual; they exemplify an artistic sense already so highly developed that it is hard to believe that they represent the earliest products of the culture to which they belong. On the other hand there is still no explanation for the finds among the Tlatilco, work in a completely different style connected with the Olmec culture on the southern coast of the Gulf of Mexico, and, even more closely, with the examples described as 'baby face'; there are points of comparison also with the stylised versions of the jaguar found in the Peruvian culture of Chavín, which led to the theory put forward by H. J. Spinden in the first place—of a 'formative interamerican horizon'.

The first great culture from the high plateau blossomed in the late phase of the preclassical period, but belongs by right to the classical period. It takes its name from the city that was certainly the most important in the Valley of Mexico during the first millennium of our era—Teotihuacán. Nothing is known of the builders or of the history of this centre with its innumerable pyramids and grandiose palaces built of sun-dried clay bricks, but we do know that its principal function must have been religious. Archaeological research has shown that its central nucleus consisted of buildings intended exclusively for the practice of religion and to the priestly caste dedicated to it. Usually the development of the culture of Teotihuacán—reckoned to last from about 300 BC to AD 900 —is subdivided into four successive phases. During the first of these periods, there was a revival in the production of terracotta vessels and figurines, of which only fragments have been found mixed with the soil used for making the large bricks for the Pyramid of the Sun. It has however been possible to reconstruct these into a type of simple pottery with geometric designs, which are either incised, painted, or negative. The small figures, more or less red in colour, belong from the stylistic point of view to the preclassical era, and according to some experts, represent ancestors venerated within the family circle; other scholars however interpret them as images of gods and symbols of fertility.

The figures of the second period are more precise and the lines re-create the flattened shape of the head found in funeral masks, either in clay or in stone. The eyes and mouth are indicated by slits, the nose is narrow, and there are enormous disc-shaped ear-rings. The third, or classical period, was marked by significant changes in the technical field. The use of moulds was introduced and the range of subjects widened to include the representation of a somewhat complex pantheon; the figures are more or less standardised, but the features are modelled with a certain delicacy. There are two basic versions: the first with a completely bald head and the second with ornaments and headgear of varying complexity. Here the wrinkled god of fire, Huehueteotl, and the god of rain, Tlaloc, make their first appearance. Typical earthenware specimens include a vessel with a long neck placed at an angle and a broad, low receptacle with a flat base, standing on three small feet and sometimes with a conical cover; on the sides it is possible to decipher a pattern of designs, either incised in low relief or in fresco, symbolising flowers, water, mountains, animals and deities. The fresco decoration is highly reminiscent in subject matter and technique of the mural paintings that decorate both the interior and exterior of the palaces of Teotihuacán, which were built at the same period. These vessels, with their varying shades of green, turquoise, pink, yellow, grey and white combining in a harmonious whole, are the products of a grasp of technique and composition; indeed, they can be counted among the masterpieces of Precolumbian ceramic art. This period was also the heyday of another type of ceramic called 'fine orange', which takes its name both from the thinness of the impasto and its beautiful colour. Its most common form is a cup, standing on a low foot and decorated with geometrical figures incised before firing. In this third period (lasting from half way through the 5th to the beginning of the 7th century AD), this powerful theocratic culture must have exerted an important influence on Mexico and even beyond—on Kaminaljuyú in Guatemala, for example, whose famous frescoes (among others) derive from the pictorial style of Teotihuacán. The fourth and last period is characterised by figurines with complicated clothing and decoration, such as the great anthropomorphous incense containers; these however are works that testify to the slow extinction of a great artistic civilisation.

22. Polychrome vessel. Height 7½ in. Cholula, State of Puebla, Mexico. Private collection, Los Angeles.

23. Xipe Totec. Height 2 ft 10 in. Alvarado, State of Veracruz, Mexico. Private collection, Milan.

22

22.   Polychrome vessel. Height 7½ in. Cholula, State of Puebla, Mexico. Private collection, Los Angeles. A typical example of Cholula ceramics, notable for its fine polychrome decoration and the rich symbolism of its motifs, which are different on every object.

23.   Xipe Totec. Height 2 ft 10 in. Alvarado, State of Veracruz, Mexico. Private collection, Milan. A representation of the Mexican god Xipe Totec, also called 'Our Lord of the Skins', for he is usually depicted with his face and body covered with the skin of a recent victim. Here, the scale-like appearance of the skin is reminiscent of another god, Quetzalcoatl, 'the plumed serpent'.

24.   God of Fire. Height 2 ft 9 in. Cerro de las Mesas, State of Veracruz, Mexico. Museo Nacional de Antropología, Mexico City. Representations of this deity are among the earliest objects produced in the Precolumbian world; they also occur in stone sculpture. The god is usually portrayed as an old man with his face deeply scored with wrinkles, carrying on his shoulders or his head a receptacle, which acts as a brazier.

25.   Figure of a priest. Height 10 in. Napiola, State of Veracruz, Mexico. Museo Nacional de Antropología, Mexico City. In this figure, the head, which is deliberately out of proportion, is carried with dignity on the tiny body. The facial features, the head-dress and the whole style of the object reflect the influence of Maya art.

24. God of Fire. Height 2 ft 9 in. Cerro de las Mesas, State of Veracruz, Mexico. Museo Nacional de Antropología, Mexico City.

25. Figure of a priest. Height 10 in. Napiola, State of
Veracruz, Mexico. Museo Nacional de Antropología,
Mexico City.

Around the 10th century, after a period of disorder and political and social change, Teotihuacán came to a sudden and obscure end. At this time, the Toltec, members of a group of warlike peoples who had come down from the northern high plateaux to conquer Central Mexico, settled in the region to the north-west of Mexico City, where they founded their capital, Tula. Here they lived until about the 13th century, the period of the Chichimec invasion, and extended their hegemony over the present-day states of Tlaxcala, Hidalgo, Morelos, Puebla, Sinaloa, Yucatán and Chiapas. This Toltec civilisation may seem sometimes to be a re-elaboration of that of Teotihuacán, but it nevertheless was marked by characteristics of its own.

Toltec ceramics have been closely studied because of their part in establishing the chronology of the period, and at Tula a wide range of types has been traced. The type known as Coyotlatelco is widespread; its most characteristic shape is a tripod cup with feet usually of rounded shape and decoration consists of geometrical motifs—undulating lines, spirals, key patterns, triangles and checks, well spaced out in red on a background of cream or yellow-grey. Another style, that of Mazapán, includes cups and dishes similar in colour to those of Coyotlatelco, but with a more simplified decoration. This is in the form of a series of lines, parallel and sinuous, traced fairly roughly on the inside of the vessels. The sculptures—female figures made from moulds—have a strangely flattened shape, which makes them look like planks, with prominent noses and extravagant adornment; they are often painted in white, red, black, yellow and turquoise. The so-called 'volcano' pottery—the first examples were found in the 19th century on the slopes of various volcanoes round Mexico City—includes vessels resembling pitchers with hand-carved handles and impasto-type reliefs (like those seen on the mask of Tlaloc) often painted in blue after firing. It was probably this culture that also produced the polychrome terracottas from Jalapazco representing the god of fire, carved by hand and painted in bright colours after firing.

The Mexica tribe, who belonged to the Chichimec group—the warlike invaders who came down from the north into the valley of Mexico in successive waves —passed through a transitional period as a collection of small nomadic groups; then, in about 1370, they succeeded in creating a centre of their own on the marshy island of Tenochtitlán, which lay in the ancient lake Texcoco. Their capital, on whose ruins Mexico City stands today, was the most important and fascinating native metropolis known to the Europeans of the period. The Aztec, as they were called, were a warlike people who succeeded in establishing fairly rapidly political domination over the greater part of Central and Southern Mexico, while culturally they assimilated many already existing and contemporary elements from the Teotihuacán and Toltec cultures and particularly from that of Mixteca-Puebla. This influence is mostly clearly seen in the pottery. For example, a variety of objects made from a yellow-coloured clay with geometric and stylised decorative motifs painted in black, had already been produced in the neighbourhood of Puebla after the year AD 900. Thus the first and second Aztec periods are in fact concerned with the artistic forms and designs that evolved before their own period; they were also affected by some of the styles developed at Tenayuca—a city only a few miles away from Tenochtitlán, which was also occupied by groups of Chichimec. Here were produced the tripod cups with black curvilinear motifs on an orange background. These motifs were stylised representations of serpents, sometimes reduced to abstract forms and executed fairly roughly. During the Third and Fourth periods, which are more genuinely Aztec, the impasto is better and more refined, the execution is more careful and the decoration, which includes more realistic themes such as birds and fishes, is more highly finished and more varied. Another type of Aztec pottery consists of vase-shaped cups and receptacles with a single conical foot, with an impasto fired at high temperature and covered in a reddish-brown colour and with motifs painted in black and white. There are also many statuettes representing the protective gods either in solid clay or hollow inside; figures represented include such gods as Quetzalcoatl, Xipe Totec, Xochiquetzal and Chalchiuhtlicue. There are large numbers of censers—some of them large—consisting of two cylindrical sections one on top of another, more or less vase-shaped and with a heavy impasto. Various utilitarian objects, such as pipes, musical instruments, and moulds complete the range of local pottery. It is evident however that the Aztec never really excelled in this form of art; they were dedicated above all to the making of large statues in stone and preferred to import the more valuable ceramics from their neighbours, in particular Cholula ware with its rich polychrome effects.

Western Mexico, which includes the vast area along the Pacific coast from the Gulf of California to the boundaries of the State of Oaxaca, has been the centre of varied and important cultures. (At present the classification and chronology of these cultures is far from clearly defined, though they will certainly be affected by research and study which are in progress today.) As far as pottery is concerned, centres of particular interest flourished in the modern states of Nayarit, Jalisco and Colima, which have given their names to the ancient local cultures. The choice of themes and the techniques employed are common to them all, as are certain distinctive characteristics that differentiate them clearly from the other cultures of the Mexican high plateau. Their style belongs to that of the preclassical period, probably because, having reached an effective stage of development at that time, their isolation caused them to retain its typical characteristics during the following period. This type of art usually finds its inspiration in subjects from everyday life, while the connection with religious symbolism

26. Figure of a young girl. Height 1 ft. Dicha Tuerta, State
of Veracruz, Mexico. Museum of the American Indian,
New York.

26.   Figure of a young girl. Height 1 ft. Dicha Tuerta, State of Veracruz, Mexico. Museum of the American Indian, New York. The open-armed gesture, the vividly expressive face and the details of the clothing make this sculpture one of the best examples of the art of Veracruz, an area rich in high quality work.

27.   Seated god of rain. Height 1 ft 8 in. Tierra Blanca, State of Veracruz, Mexico. Private collection, Milan. The powerful impact of this extraordinary piece of sculpture is created by the simplification of the shapes and the severity of the composition. The rings around the eyes symbolise clouds, and the serpent's teeth represent the earth.

28.   Urn with figure in relief. Height 2 ft 8 in. State of Veracruz, Mexico. Private collection, Milan. An urn dominated by the figure of an aristocratic warrior modelled in high relief with great refinement and strength.

29.   Effigy vessel. Height 17 in. State of San Luis Potosí, Mexico. Museo Nacional de Antropología, Mexico City. This example, in cream with black decoration, is typical of the ceramics produced by this culture during the last phase before the Spanish conquest.

30.   God of Fire. Height 1 ft. Toluca, State of Mexico. Museum of the American Indian, New York. One of the best examples of 'fine orange' ceramics. The god is represented with surprising care and sensitivity, and is skilfully fused with the large spherical urn on its back.

27.   Seated god of rain. Height 1 ft 8 in. Tierra Blanca State of Veracruz, Mexico. Private collection, Milan.

28. Urn with figure in relief. Height 2 ft 8 in. State of Veracruz, Mexico. Private collection, Milan.

29. Effigy vessel. Height 17 in. State of San Luis Potosí, Mexico. Museo Nacional de Antropología, Mexico City.

67

30. God of Fire. Height 1 ft. Toluca, State of Mexico.
Museum of the American Indian, New York.

that occurs so frequently in other Mexican cultures seems to be absent. The clay is carved and baked in the shapes of both figures and vessels, with a technical mastery that permits the manufacture of objects, often of large dimensions; these were all used as funerary offerings and were buried with the dead. In the state of Nayarit, and in particular in the southern part of Ixtlán del Rio, discoveries include a large number of grotesque human figures; as a rule, accurate anatomical proportions are purposely ignored while certain physical characteristics are exaggerated. In addition to isolated and hollowed out figures there are also groups in solid clay, somewhat summarily executed, representing scenes from daily life— dances, games, and so on, in which typical local buildings can often be seen. A chronological order has been tentatively suggested, based on various individual points of style—for example the way eyes are represented: the primitive type of 'coffee-bean' eye was followed by a swollen type cut by a narrow slit; finally the problem was solved with greater anatomical realism. The terracotta is brown and painted in various shades of red; on this is superimposed a geometrical decoration in black, yellow, cream, greenish white and brown, which brings out details of the clothing or ornamentation. Apart from these anthropomorphous representations, a vast range of pottery with the same ornamental characteristics has been identified.

Objects originating in the neighbouring state of Jalisco, although they have features not unlike those of Nayarit and Colima work (which is sometimes difficult to identify) express a different aesthetic concept: the lack of proportion, especially in the limbs, seems to result from a desire to exaggerate a gesture or a piece of clothing rather than to present a grotesquely deformed image; the head is unusually elongated, while the eyes are large and conspicuous, the nose slender and the wide mouth is open. The figures are generally grey-cream in colour and large in size. Men—including soldiers—and women are represented in a sober and tranquil style that gives them a remote and concentrated expression.

Colima ceramics are distinguished by their individual colouring, a fine brilliant red, by the greater accuracy of their execution and by their sophisticated appearance produced by their beautifully smooth and rounded shapes. There is a notable variety of subjects, but the human or animal figures are always treated with a definite respect for their natural shape: men and women in a surprising variety of costumes are portrayed with serene and often cheerful expressions. There are many representations of hunchbacks, dwarfs, soldiers, dancer-acrobats, old men, water-carriers, drinkers; the variety of expressions makes them seem almost like portraits, though they are in fact no more than life-like sketches. Animals and birds are also depicted in large numbers: parrots, ducks, pelicans, armadillos and most of all dogs—the Techico breed, smooth-haired and reared to be eaten—are subjects that recur constantly and reveal the artists' deep and sensitive power of observation. In addition to isolated figures (which are not always in the usual dark red colour, but range from cream to brown), there are groups of people modelled in solid clay, not unlike some of the Nayarit groups. There are also many vessels, again in a wide variety of shapes; a particularly unusual type is that modelled like a giant pumpkin supported on three feet.

Our information about the earliest artistic period of the state of Michoacán, also in western Mexico, is still vague, partly because an Indian people called the Tarasca, who settled there in about the 10th century, has made research into the preceding periods particularly complicated and for years has led to the misapplication of the term 'Tarasca' to all forms of art in western Mexico during ancient times. Today however it has been shown that forms of pre-Tarasca culture existed in the area; for example, one of the most advanced expressions of the preclassical culture had its centre in Chupícuaro—a vast cemetery on the borders between the states of Michoacán and Guanajuato, where the most ancient ceramics seem to coincide with the second Ticomán period (500 BC-AD 300); further, many discoveries contemporary with the Zacatenco period in the valley of Mexico (before 500 BC) have been made in El Opeño, the most ancient centre known in this state. The tombs have yielded enormously rich finds of polished terracotta vessels, both in black and reddish brown, showing an advanced standard of technique and always decorated in several colours with rectilinear geometrical motifs with incised figurative designs; negative painting is peculiar to Chupícuaro ceramics. There are also very many terracottas with anthropomorphous subjects, which are either hollow and on a large scale—in bright red with a prominent zig-zag decoration in black and white—or small and solid, somewhat flattened and in opaque and light-coloured clay, modelled by hand and decorated with the addition of clay pastilles intended to represent necklaces and adornments; those which are characterised by deeply slanting 'coffee-bean' eyes seem to be older in date.

Just as Teotihuacán was the cultural centre of the Mexican plateau, so another city, which took the name Monte Albán from the locality where it stood, became the seat of the more important culture that developed in the state of Oaxaca, in southern Mexico. Nothing is known of the people who founded this city—probably about the 8th or 7th century BC—but it became the religious centre of the Zapotec, the largest local ethnic group. Monte Albán preserved traces of a long occupation dating from the preclassical era; its artistic evolution is subdivided, according to the research carried out by Alfonso Caso, into five successive stages. The first Monte Albán period is represented by vessels and small figures in terracotta, modelled in the vigorous manner typical of the preclassical period. In particular the vessels show a technical skill and an extraordinary beauty of decoration in which the design is partly modelled in

31. Urn with a carved figure. Height 1 ft 11 in. Mayapán, State of Yucatán, Mexico. Museo Nacional de Antropología, Mexico City.

31. Urn with a carved figure. Height 1 ft 11 in. Mayapán, State of Yucatán, Mexico. Museo Nacional de Antropología, Mexico City. This figure carved in relief represents a priest. Many urns and censers of this type have been found in Mayapán, the city-state that more-or-less dominated Yucatán from the 13th to the mid-15th century; they are characterised by elaborate decorative detail.

32. Cylindrical container. Height 4 ft. Palenque, State of Chiapas, Mexico. Museo Nacional de Antropología, Mexico City. These hollow, tubular terracottas (which were probably used in funeral rites) are usually richly decorated with symbolic motifs carved in relief; few traces remain of their original vivid polychrome colours. The face in the centre is that of the sun god.

33. Censer with lid. Height 10 in. Dipartimento di El Quiché, Guatemala. Private collection, Los Angeles. The lower part includes a somewhat rough representation of a face; on the lid are four fine modelled heads with typical Maya features.

34. Xipe Totec. Height 3 ft 7 in. Xolalpán, State of Mexico. Museo Nacional de Antropología, Mexico City. This deity not only symbolises spring, the harvest and the idea of renewal but also, as the god of fallen warriors and sacrificial stones, represents sacrifice and penitence—that is, the Purification of souls. On top of the head are three fine star symbols. This work, which was discovered in the Teotihuacán area, shows a clear Maya-Toltec influence.

32. Cylindrical container. Height 4 ft. Palenque, State of Chiapas, Mexico. Museo Nacional de Antropología, Mexico City.

33. Censer with lid. Height 10 in. Dipartimento de El Quiché, Guatemala. Private collection, Los Angeles.

34. Xipe Totec. Height 3 ft 7 in. Xolalpán, State of Mexico.
Museo Nacional de Antropología, Mexico City.

relief and partly incised: many of these, which reproduce human, animal or divine subjects, show an obvious Olmec influence. The second period saw the development and perfection of the technique of the preceding era; it is also largely concerned with the creation of sculpture in terracotta, also of large dimensions, of such majesty and aesthetic quality that the resulting product is in a class of its own. Many of these works are figures with Olmec-type features wearing ornaments indicating their high social rank; often they hold their hands raised in front of their chests with the palms turned outwards, presumably in some sort of gesture of rejection. In addition there are funerary urns that are not simple and unadorned types of vessel but resemble sculpture that is truly commemorative of the dead, enriched with magnificently modelled details. This second period shows to an even greater extent the influence of the cultures from the coast of the Gulf of Mexico, preclassical Maya and central America, either in the shape or in the iconography. The third period is primarily influenced by Teotihuacán art, even if the local style tends to make its elegant artistry somewhat ponderous; towards the end of this period the use of moulds was introduced. The large funerary urns represent, in a particularly elaborate style, gods and goddesses, animals—bats and jaguars are popular subjects—and human beings; the latter are seated, following the classical Teotihuacán and Maya style, their legs crossed and their hands resting on their knees. The period of

Monte Albán decadence occurred during the fourth period. This decadent quality is also apparent in the ceramics, which are more stereotyped, are weighed down with a superabundance of ornament and show a gradual decrease of vitality and vigour; the impasto also is proportionately rougher. The fourth and last period is clearly influenced by the Mixtec culture, which began to emerge at the end of the third Monte Albán period (about the 7th century AD) and with the Aztec culture continued until the Spanish conquest.

The rise of the Mixtec culture is also obscure; it probably originated in the north-west of the state of Oaxaca, close to the Puebla culture, at a date that is still being debated by scholars, and probably had its most important centre in the city of Mitla, where there are many buildings rich in wall mosaics. On the other hand, the presence of this culture affected the whole field of central American art in the post-classical era. Monte Albán itself reveals traces perhaps of an occupation but certainly of a Mixtec influence. The first terracottas are largely related to those of the first Monte Albán periods; it is not until about the year 1000 that the more typical monochrome ceramics (in black and grey) appeared, followed by the two-coloured variety often decorated with motifs and ornaments in vermilion, black and brown on a white background. But the most beautiful terracottas are those that record in their decoration the illustrations to the famous codices, which have made this culture so widely known: geometrical motifs, key-patterns, curves, spirals and scrolls mingle with flowers, deities, hieroglyphs and animals, painted in very bright colours on particularly vivid backgrounds; the combination of colours includes brown painted over red, yellow and white on grey, black, yellow and red on white, light brown on black, blue, black and silvergrey on red. There are many examples of a deep cup with carved feet representing the heads of serpents or eagles. Cholula, in the state of Puebla, is the centre with the richest production and the highest aesthetic standard; the work found there includes great cylindrical jars with hollow bases, braziers for incense, small perfume-burners, dishes of various types and several portrait-vases. There are at least four different types of technique, including, during the classical period, a stucco-type decoration applied after firing similar to that used in Teotihuacán and Kaminaljuyú. After the classical period there appeared a type of lacquered ceramic, which remained in use for several centuries; the colour was added after a first baking on a layer of gesso-like substance, which was polished and then fired; orange, brown, black, blue, red and white are used in various combinations. The most usual decorative subjects include serpents, flowers, feathers, eagles, waves, volutes, skulls and crossbones, glyphs and human and animal faces. From the region of Calipan and Teotihuacán in the state of Puebla come numerous small pieces of sculpture in terracotta, with fresco type polychrome motifs, which seem to be mostly representations of gods.

The coastal plains covered with dense forests that extend along the Gulf of Mexico include three major areas of archaeological interest. The southern regions of the state of Veracruz and the state of Tabasco were the recognised centre of the famous Olmec culture, the first to acquire as early as the preclassical period both a definite importance and skill and a well-defined character, unlike the more primitive groups existing at the same period in Mexico. This culture in fact emerged during that long period of preclassical preparation involving both Mexico and Central America, and it is regarded by many students as partly responsible for the classical civilisations of Central America, including the Teotihuacán, Maya and Zapotec. The presence of Olmec-style objects in a preclassical village was brought to light for the first time by the excavations carried out by George and Susannah Vaillant in Gualupita in the state of Morelos; other discoveries followed, including the extremely important find in Tlatilco (under the direction of Miguel Covarrubias) of tomb offerings, which revealed, as in Gualupita, the presence of figurines contemporary in style to those from El Arbolillo and Zacatenco and also showed the influence of a totally extraneous style, that of the Olmec. During recent years the excavations carried out at Tlapacoya (Mexico) and Las Bocas (Puebla) have notably enriched the Olmec cultural heritage and have underlined the importance and diffusion of this culture in the preclassical era. The most typical Olmec centres were Tres Zapotes—which

35. Figure of a man. Height 8½ in. Jaina. State of Campeche, Mexico. Private Collection. Washington.

36. Cylindrical polychrome vessel. Height 8½ in. Jaina, State of Campeche, Mexico. Museo Nacional de Antropología, Mexico City.

35.   Figure of a man. Height 8½ in. Jaina, State of Campeche, Mexico. Private Collection. This small masterpiece, made of solid stone, perhaps represents an orator of high status and prestige exhorting an imaginary audience. Note the clothing, the headdress and the pectoral, which are rich and complex, also the cheeks and chin covered with a kind of mask.

36.   Cylindrical polychrome vessel. Height 8½ in. Jaina, State of Campeche, Mexico. Museo Nacional de Antropología, Mexico City. Because of their rich variety of themes, sumptuous polychrome colouring, refined design and finally harmonious composition, Maya vessels rank among the finest earthenware ever produced; the emphasis on pictorial decoration led to a preference for cylindrical sides, on which designs could spread themselves without interruption.

37.   Vessel with decoration in relief. Height 7 in. San Augustin Acasaguastlan, Dipartimento di Zacapa, Guatemala. Museum of the American Indian, New York. This vessel, which is outstanding both from a technical and an aesthetic point of view, is undoubtedly the work of a master-potter. It is a fine example of the application in Maya earthenware work of the technique of decoration in relief, which is carved in the clay before firing.

38.   Cylindrical polychrome vessel. Height 8 in. Dipartimento di Guatemala, Guatemala. Private collection, Los Angeles. Another cylindrical vessel, one of the shapes most frequently found in Maya ceramics. Here the fresco technique has been used to produce an abstraction of motifs and a juxtaposition of colours that give the decoration an almost modern appearance.

37. Vessel with decoration in relief. Height 7 in. San Agustin Acasaguastlan, Dipartimento di Zacapa, Guatemala. Museum of the American Indian, New York.

38. Cylindrical polychrome vessel. Height 8 in. Dipartimento di Guatemala, Guatemala. Private collection, Los Angeles.

produced discoveries dating from the period 400 BC to about AD 600—La Venta, which flourished almost alone in the preclassical era (about 800-400 BC), and San Lorenzo. Although most of the art produced consisted of sculpture in stone, terracotta still played a fairly important part and clearly belongs to an older artistic tradition. The offerings found in the tombs include many human figures and vessels; the former show well-defined and consistent characteristics, such as a solid and heavy physical structure, a full face tending to recede towards the temples, eyes of Mongolian appearance with heavy lids, and a pointed nose with wide nostrils. The most outstanding feature is the shape of the mouth, which is open, revealing the gums, while the broad, flattened upper lip is raised in a cat-like grimace; the corners of the mouth turn down threateningly, so that the lower lip forms a deep curve. This type of mouth is so characteristic that it has been defined as the 'Olmec mouth', and the plump, child-like little figure has been nicknamed 'baby face'. The most significant discoveries of these sculptured figures have been found as Las Bocas. These unusual figures, modelled in creamy-white clay and hollow inside, may possibly represent a supreme Olmec deity, the offspring of a feline father and a human mother. There are vessels in a wide variety of shapes, some cylindrical and others in the form of dishes, bottles, people or animals. The decoration consists of simple incisions, partly in relief, or of a special treatment of the surface with alternately polished and rough areas and covered with a coral red. The predominant motifs are jaguar heads and claws, largely stylised and sometimes combined with bird and scroll designs. The colours of the clay are brown, red-brown, black and creamy-white. Typical of Tlatilco and Las Bocas is a particularly fine impasto coloured white, which has been called kaolin ceramic: it is usually used in vessels and bowls without necks or in low dishes with spouts, occasionally decorated in red. The animal shapes—ducks and fish are commonest—are usually in black or brown impasto with incised decorative details and some areas scraped out.

A second important culture in the Gulf of Mexico area flourished about 300-900 AD in the northern, central and southern coastal areas of what is now the state of Veracruz. This region lay between Papantla to the north and Mistequilla to the south and had its centre at Tajín, which rivalled in magnificence Uxmal, Monte Albán and Copán. The preclassical styles here are largely similar to those of the Mexican valley, but during the classical period there developed an individual culture. Research (which is far from being complete) has as yet failed to supply a complete picture, but discoveries made so far indicate that there probably existed a transitional style between the preclassical Olmec culture and the classical culture of Veracruz; this period, moreover, was a time of extremely active cultural interchange. Teotihuacán influence is apparent in both technique and subject matter—in, for example, the representations of foreign gods and the famous fresco painting on tripod vessels. The effect of Olmec culture and that of the Maya regions and western Guatemala can also be seen. Sculpture, either in stone or terracotta, provided the highest expression of Veracruz art; the figures, both human and divine, are modelled in clay covered with a white plaster and reflect a high standard of technique and expressiveness. The first known objects are the 'smiling faces'—originating from the Mistequilla region—so-called because of their open, smiling mouths and faces; these heads, made from moulds with hand-made details added later, have characteristically flattened heads and headgear decorated with glyphs and scrolls; they are quite unlike the hand-carved figurines from Ranchito de las Animas, dating from the classical period, but probably made a little earlier. More recent excavations have revealed the existence also of complete figures representing young men and girls, their naked bodies modelled with considerable realism and with the same smiling faces, which are in striking contrast to the gallery of preoccupied or even gloomy expressions found in ancient Mexican art. Recent research in the Remojadas region of central Veracruz has uncovered another style with individual characteristics: portrait-vessels and small human or animal figures, often decorated with black bitumen, as well as representations of men and gods of considerable size, with highly expressive faces, wearing extremely magnificent garments; the ornaments they wear are often elaborate,

40. Polychrome vessel with human effigy in relief. Height 4½ in. Province of Guanacaste, Costa Rica. American Museum of Natural History, New York.

39.   Tripod vessel. Height 9 in. Island of Chiara, Gulf of Nicoya, Costa Rica. Musée de l'Homme, Paris. This type of vessel is very frequently found in Central America where there are fairly close artistic links between the various cultures. Works from Costa Rica, for example, have much in common with those produced in Nicaragua. The jaguar, a favourite decorative subject in Central American art, is repeated here in relief at the top of each foot.

40.   Polychrome vessel with human effigy in relief. Height $4\frac{1}{2}$ in. Province of Guanacaste, Costa Rica. American Museum of Natural History, New York. A common type of Costa Rican vessel with an elongated carved body resting on a hollow support. This example has an unusual type of decoration in relief representing a human face.

41.   Figure seated on a footstool. Height 9 in. Barba, Costa Rica. Musée de l'Homme, Paris. An outstanding feature of Costa Rican ceramics is the decoration, which is derived from Maya and Mexican sources. The strong geometrical motifs are brightly painted in black and reddish-brown on a cream-coloured background.

41. Figure seated on a footstool. Height 9 in. Barba, Costa
Rica. Musée de l'Homme, Paris.

while the decorative details are numerous and multi-coloured.

The northern zone of the Gulf Coast—from Papantla northwards—was the home of the Huasteco ethnic group (which has many affinities with the Maya) and is noted for stone statuary. As far as ceramics are concerned, excavations have established a succession of six different stylistic periods: the first and second date back to a preclassical period and are characterised by little figures in terracotta and vessels in black and red clay, which could be related to the work of the Maya low plateau and to the first two Monte Albán periods; the third and fourth periods belong to the classical era during which the little terracotta figures acquire a notably refined and elegant character while obvious Teotihuacán influence can be seen in the earthenware vessels. The last two periods belong to the historic era lasting from the end of the classical period to the arrival of the Spanish conquerors and is associated with the Toltec and Mixtec cultures at first, and with the Aztec culture towards the end; the recurrent decorative theme is a design of symmetrical scrolls in black on a white ground, symbolising smoke and linked with the figure of Mixcoatl, god of fire.

The Yucatán peninsula was the centre of one of the more important civilisations in the whole of the American continent. The Maya people, who were its architects, possessed such powers of observation and such technical perfection in both the scientific and artistic fields that they have earned themselves the title of the 'Greeks of America'. Their culture spread over an extremely wide area which included the present day states of Yucatán, Quintana Roo, Campeche, Tabasco, eastern Chiapas and, beyond the borders of Mexico, Guatemala, Belize, Honduras and El Salvador. Chronologically, its purely classical period—that is, unaffected by outside influences—began during the Christian era about AD 1000. Although ceramics were not the most important form of art produced by this culture, they nevertheless represent an extremely interesting aspect because of their number, variety and quality. Most of the major finds dating from the classical period were made in Guatemala; simple figurines and vessels in terracotta (belonging to the Las Charcas and Miraflores periods on the Pacific coast and to the Mamon and Chicanel periods on the low plains in the centre and to the north) show signs of preclassical influence and probably derive from the Mexican plateau. One of the most important centres of the Mamon style was Uaxactún in the Petén area, where large globular-shaped vessels and tripod containers of grey or cream-coloured clay have been found. The best examples of Las Charcas and Miraflores work come from Kaminaljuyú, which is near the present-day capital. The Mamon-style discoveries are reminiscent of those of Tlatilco, but the subsequent Chicanel period is characterised by a more original local style, whose only ceramics were containers; the decoration, which is richly coloured, is made by incision and the addition of separate parts added to the clay. During the following period, however, ceramics attained their maximum splendour. The styles became varied and the decoration, which was painted before firing, assumed major importance; the frequently brilliant effect is probably achieved by a kind of lacquer covering of organic origin. Another technique of the time was the application of a thin layer of stucco or clay as the base for the colour and incised decoration. Although the shapes of the vessels and the fresco method of colouring them were possibly imported from the centre of Mexican culture, the subject matter and curvilinear form were typically Maya. The shapes of the vessels are more or less uniform: cups, dishes with and without supports, jars of varying sizes, hemispherical bowls, cylindrical containers with three or four feet, anthropomorphous vessels with vigorous modelling. During the classical period the decorations became even richer and more beautiful: the early monochrome and geometrical designs gave way to the use of colour and naturalistic motifs. The colours included red, yellow, black and white on an orange background; ornamental designs, such as glyphs and scenes depicting historical and religious subjects, were represented more and more skilfully. Incense burners, both anthropomorphous and composite in style, are found in large numbers; they consisted of two parts—one on top of the other —and were painted in several colours. They are known to have existed at the start of the classical period, and

42. Vessel representing a jaguar. Height 4½ in. Length 10 in. Buenos Aires, Costa Rica. Private collection, Milan.

42. Vessel representing a jaguar. Height 4½ in. Length 10 in. Buenos Aires, Costa Rica. Private collection, Milan. In Central American iconography, the jaguar is sometimes represented in fierce and realistic guise, at others it is so conventionalised and simplified as to be unrecognisable. Here the beast appears tamed, perhaps partly because of the harmonious geometrical decoration.

43. Three-legged vessel representing a jaguar. Height 1 ft 2 in. El General, Province of Puntarenas, Costa Rica. Museum of the American Indian, New York. Here the head and lower limbs of the jaguar are represented in the round while the polychrome decoration is limited to carefully demarcated areas in a way typical of many terracottas from Costa Rica.

44. Polychrome vessel with a rattle. Height 10 in. Province of Guanacaste, Costa Rica. Private collection, Los Angeles. An example of one of the shapes that recur in Central American ceramic art. Often pellets of clay are inserted into the object—here, in the base—which make a noise when shaken. The dense decoration is made up of stylised jaguar and plumed serpent motifs.

43. Three-legged vessel representing a jaguar. Height 1 ft 2 in. El General, Province of Puntarenas, Costa Rica, Museum of the American Indian, New York.

44. Polychrome vessel with a rattle. Height 10 in. Province of Guanacaste, Costa Rica. Private collection, Los Angeles.

they are found in many areas both in Mexico and Guatemala. Towards the end of this period, human beings and animals are regularly represented in ceramic painting. Among the best works are Chama vessels, on which the polychrome figures, bordered with a precise and elegant black line, stand out boldly. A further stage of technical and stylistic skill was achieved by the stylised clay statuettes, made either by hand or with moulds or by a combination of both methods. Fine examples of these have come to light in the Palenque and Jonutan regions, but the most outstanding for quality and refinement are the finds in the cemetery of Jaina, a small island facing the state of Campeche. Most of the figures are between six and ten inches high, but their proportions are so perfect that they seem larger. They are made of a fine orange clay, covered with a whitish plaster with traces of blue and yellow ochre colouring. Noblemen, priests and matrons are shown in various attitudes, either standing or sitting; the complicated dress and ornaments are represented with great precision. A whole range of physical types, from young to old, some normally healthy, others deformed, provide a series of lifelike portraits executed with intelligence and elegance. The variations in style, which are reasonably marked, reveal a chronological succession of at least three phases, all included within the classical period. During the post-classical one that followed, the major centres of artistic interest shifted to the peninsula of Yucatán from the mountainous regions of Guatemala and the thickly wooded areas of Petén. The cylindrical vessels are decorated with a form of low relief, achieved by scooping out the lower level of the surface (as had already been done in the late classical period). Decorative additions were also made by means of moulds. In addition, there was a fairly widespread output of 'plumbate' ceramics, which stylistically were of Mexican origin and were mainly used for ceremonial purposes. Quantities of censers and large funerary urns of complex construction, depicting gods and nobles and decorated with a large amount of detail, have been found in Mayapán, the city-state that dominated Yucatán from 1200 to 1450 following the period of Toltec supremacy. The final Maya period in art is characterised by polychrome ceramics: vessels, usually globular in shape, with two handles stamped with heads of feline animals, or bowls, always decorated with a geometrical design.

Central America to the south of the Maya region can be regarded as the meeting-point of the two principal artistic currents, the Mexican and the Andean. However, precise and detailed information about this region is scanty, since archaeological research is still incomplete. The four states that make up the region today—Honduras, Nicaragua, Costa Rica and Panama—reflect a variety of influences, some Maya or Mexican, others, particularly during the initial and final periods, South American. Ceramics, which were always characterised by a particular type of polychrome colouring, provide evidence of a continuity of style from Honduras to Panama; the basic colours are red and black on a cream-coloured background and the range of shapes is well-defined. Simple globular vessels are common, sometimes with spouts; other work comprises cups with or without pedestals or with three or four legs, and vessels in human and animal shape. The decoration is incised, modelled and sometimes in the form of human masks or the heads, tails or claws of animals in relief. Designs in colour include bands of drawings incorporating stylised and sometimes highly abstract human and animal motifs—alligators, serpents, jaguars, monkeys. There are also some human figurines of the pre-classical Mexican type and various musical instruments.

Honduras—more so than any other region except perhaps some typically Maya zones such as Copán—is characterised by a mixture of styles with different origins. Some are clearly Maya, as is shown by the cylindrical vessels from Santa Rita, in which rich polychrome figurative designs stand out against an orange background. In complete contrast is the absolutely geometrical decoration of vessels with a conical body and two small handles with strongly stylised motifs on surfaces that have been specially prepared before firing. At Playa de los Muertos stratigraphic excavations have revealed vessels and monochrome figurines of somewhat plain design in layers below those containing polychrome ceramics.

Nicaragua and Costa Rica constitute a more or less complete cultural unit. Both the Costa Rican penin-

45. Funerary urn. Height 1 ft 5 in. Rio Tabasara, Province
of Chiriquí, Panama. Museum of the American Indian,
New York.

46. Cup on a tall stand. Height 10 in. Province of Veraguas, Panama. Museum of the American Indian, New York.

45.   Funerary urn. Height 1 ft 5 in. Rio Tabasara, Province of Chiriquí, Panama. Museum of the American Indian, New York. The shape and design of this vessel are rare in Panamanian art, though the warm colours and the black line surrounding the pattern are typical features of this locality.

46.   Cup on a tall stand. Height 10 in. Province of Veraguas, Panama. Museum of the American Indian, New York. An example of the most typical shape found in Panamanian ceramics. The decoration, based on extremely stylised animal motifs and dominated by symmetrically arranged curving lines, is equally characteristic.

47.   Vessel with emblem of the crocodile-god. Height 8 in. Province of Veraguas, Panama. Museum of the American Indian, New York. The full round shape of this vessel is accentuated by the fantastic decoration in red and black on a buff-coloured background. The image of the god, depicted in a graphic and surprisingly modern manner, dramatically conveys the menacing quality of divine power.

48.   Hunchback figure. Height 1 ft 3½ in. Andrés, District of San Domingo, Dominican Republic. Museum of the American Indian, New York. Thought to be the image of a god since it was found on an altar, this figure is an outstanding example of West Indian work both technically—because of the extremely thin clay walls—and aesthetically.

47. Vessel with emblem of the crocodile-god. Height 8 in. Province of Veraguas, Panama. Museum of the American Indian, New York.

48. Hunchback figure. Height 1 ft 3½ in. Andrés, District of San Domingo, Dominican Republic. Museum of the American Indian, New York.

sula of Nicoya and the Pacific coast of Nicaragua are noted for oval-shaped vessels and cups standing on a hollowed-out foot or on three legs often in animal shape and for cylindrical and tripod vessels decorated with stylised motifs based on human and animal figures in a richly polychrome design that derived, like many of the forms, from the Maya and Mexican cultures. Boldly modelled shapes in relief are a fairly common feature of this work. The ceramics of the central high plateau, while including a polychrome type very similar to that found on the coast (in both the decoration is predominantly geometrical) largely consist of monochrome earthenware, brown or red in colour, with incised or modelled decoration. This difference in styles probably reflects a difference in period: the products of the interior probably precede the Nicoya style, which cannot be dated earlier than the late classical period either by the presence of contemporary Maya decoration or by the discovery of Nicoya ceramics in the deposits at Copán belonging to the middle and late classical period. On the other hand, an obvious Mixtec influence, evident both in certain shapes and in certain types of decoration and techniques, probably means that the Nicoya discoveries date from the period 500-1300.

Four archaeological regions, each with a reasonably distinctive style, have been located in Panama, of which, from an artistic point of view, only Chiriquí, Veraguas and Coclé are important. The first, which has links with southern Costa Rica, produced relatively small globular vessels, either undecorated or with semicircular bands enclosing vertical motifs in negative or in black and red on white. The Coclé and Veraguas regions are notable for a strong South American influence; typical Coclé products are dishes and cups, either rectangular or hollowed out with circular supports, and globular vessels with bottle-shaped mouths or rectangular bodies and hollow necks. The decoration, which is of high quality and almost always polychrome—black and red on a cream-coloured background—is characterised by a surprising richness of curvilinear motifs. A horizontal S-shaped pattern with an intermittent zig-zag line and embellished with scrolls is found in many examples from the earliest period onwards; decorative subjects include animals of various kinds—crocodiles, birds, tortoises, crabs, monkeys—whose characteristics are sometimes merged with those of human beings, producing motifs with a strangely surrealistic appearance. On the figurative and portrait-vessels, some details, such as the head and the hands, are painted while others, such as the feet and the nose, are in relief.

In contrast, ceramics from Veraguas which include many different shapes, usually lack any pictorial decoration, although patterns are sometimes carved and incised, or applied, as on the portrait-vessels; there are however polychrome examples, in which red predominates as the basic colour used in conjunction with black and pale cream. Stylised decorative patterns mostly representing animals are also used.

49. Warrior seated on a stool. Height 9 in. Alto Cauca area, Colombia. Musée de l'Homme, Paris.

50. Lid of urn with human figure. Height 1 ft 2 in. Rio Sinú, Tumaco region, Columbia. Museo de Antropología, Bogotá.

51. Ocarina carved in human shape. Height 9½ in.
Dipartimento di Nariño, Colombia. Museo de Antropología,
Bogotá.

113

49. Warrior seated on a stool. Height 9 in. Alto Cauca area, Colombia. Musée de l'Homme, Paris. Such representations of warriors are typical of the discoveries made in the tombs in the Alto region of the Cauca river. The shield, the complex and impressive crest, the ferocious attitude or—as in this example—the air of concentration give these works a highly individual appearance.

50. Lid of urn with human figure. Height 1 ft 2 in. Rio Sinú, Tumaco region, Colombia. Museo de Antropología, Bogotá. The realistic quality of this example is rare in Colombian art, in which human figures are often represented in unnatural attitudes or, even more frequently, stylised or distorted to the point of grotesqueness.

51. Ocarina carved in human shape. Height $9\frac{1}{2}$ in. Dipartimento di Nariño, Colombia. Museo de Antropología, Bogotá. Bells and wind instruments always provided the Precolumbian artist with an excuse to give free rein to his imagination; for this reason, the instrument's aesthetic quality is almost always superior to its practical value.

52. Mask of an old man. Height 10 in. Tumaco region, Colombia. Museo de Antropología, Bogotá. The equatorial Pacific coast can be seen as the last outpost of Central American and Mexican artistic traditions, with which links with the art of the central Andes are slender. The terracotta mask, for example, is unknown in all purely South American art.

52. Mask of an old man. Height 10 in. Tumaco region, Colombia. Museo de Antropología, Bogotá.

THE ANDEAN CULTURES

The mountain range running from Colombia southwards along the Pacific coast has been the home of
various cultures, which, in spite of their many different styles, have certain basic features in common. The
most obvious of these are the rarity of human representation in the sculpture and the tendency to distort
the human body whenever it is used as a decorative
motif, either by giving it a grotesque appearance or
treating it in an exaggeratedly stylised manner.

The regions crossed by the Magdalena and Cauca
rivers have been the source of the major archaeological finds in Colombia. It is to this area in fact that
the cultures of San Agustin, Quimbaya, Tierradento,
Mosquito, the Alto Cauca, Chibcha and Tairona
belong. Clearly defined characteristics are evident in
the Quimbaya funerary terracottas, which include
cups, double-bodied vessels of typically Peruvian appearance in the shapes of animals or birds and large
amphora and vessels; also anthropomorphous statuettes both small and large, decorated in black, red and
white, or with negative painting in two or three
colours, or with incisions, or with extra parts added
afterwards or shown in relief while the background is
left blank. Where human figures are included the head
is usually represented as a rectangle with the longer
side as the base, while the eyes and mouth are mere
incisions.

The Chibcha, who lived in the neighbourhood of

present-day Bogotá, constituted a true state (in the modern sense of the word) headed by an absolute monarch. Their terracottas, which are greyish in colour and unpolished, include containers—cups, vessels on supporting feet, and anthropomorphous vessels in which the full, rounded part represents the body and the mouthpiece, the head—and small figures in a rough, red impasto, which, though inaccurate as portrayals of the human body have a remarkable expressive power; the eyes are in the form of closed eyelids and an ornament hangs from the nose, often concealing the mouth.

The only finds associated with the Mosquito culture, which was located in the forests of the central reaches of the Magdalena river, are cylindrical terracotta funerary urns. On their lids are seated human figures with their legs apart and their hands resting on their knees: the foreheads recede, their eyes are slits and their noses and ears pronounced. In the upper reaches of the Cauca river two categories of objects have been discovered in many tombs: globular monochrome vessels in red clay with or without supporting feet, often with the addition of motifs in relief, and, more rarely, figures representing a warrior with a raised shield seated on a small throne; he wears a tall helmet, and on his back he carries a stylised animal, probably symbolising his 'double', that is, his *alter ego* or his spiritual protector.

In Ecuador, in the province of Carchi on the borders of Colombia, various types of vessels have been found fairly deeply buried in tombs. These include an interesting oval-shaped urn with a neck hollowed out and a round base, which is strongly reinforced, suggesting that it may have been buried in the ground; the most usual type of decoration is a geometrical motif painted in red on a cream-coloured background, or else negative painting with motifs in black on a red or cream background. These urns are very similar to the Inca *aryballoi,* which were widespread in Peru. From the plateaux in the south come large terracotta cylinders, drums and seats, which may have been influenced by the Maya. The Guengala figurines, from the province of Guayas, are easily recognisable; they are hand-made in the shape of a whistle in red clay with an incised rectangular decoration at the joints of the arms and legs. Similar figures were produced by the Manabí and Esmeraldas cultures. The moulded figurines from the Esmeraldas region are perhaps later, however, although those with the distinctive 'coffee-bean' eyes (which are also found at Manabí) are earlier, if we apply the same criterion of classification as is used for Mexico; Maya and Central American influences are often apparent in the ornaments and the delicacy of the detail. The vessels, many of which are conical or in the form of a tripod cup, are simple and usually small with incised and sculpted decoration, sometimes painted in red. A unique tradition— and one that is quite distinct both from that of the northern Andes and that of the low plains of South America—closely links the numerous cultures that

53. Vessel representing two animals. Height 8½ in.
Dipartimento di Antioquia, Colombia. Museo de Antropología,
Bogotá.

54. Crouching figure. Height 11 in. Dipartimento di Antioquia,
Colombia. Museo de Antropología, Bogotá.

53.   Vessel representing two animals. Height 8½ in. Dipartimento di Antioquia, Colombia. Museo de Antropología, Bogotá.
The many funerary vessels from the area midway along the
Cauca river are characterised by such a rich variety of forms,
styles and techniques, that they may possibly belong to a succession of cultural periods; this theory however is not yet completely accepted by scholars. This example belongs to the
Quimbaya culture.

54.   Crouching figure. Height 11 in. Dipartimento di Antio-
quoia, Colombia. Museo de Antropología, Bogotá. The figure
has been simplified in various ways: the body is in the shape of
a conical trunk shape, the limbs tubular, the face mask-like,
although not lacking in expression. Indeed, this treatment
might be said to increase the work's intensity.

55.   Vessel in human shape. Height 9½ in. El Angel, Ecuador.
Musée de l'Homme, Paris. This figure, unrealistically portrayed
as a large deformed egg, is obviously the product of a powerful
imagination. The limbs are represented in a simplified manner
and appear more animal than human; in violent contrast is the
expression of the face, which is intense and almost ecstatic.

55. Vessel in human shape. Height 9½ in. El Angel, Ecuador.
Musée de l'Homme, Paris.

developed in the central area of the Andes, including the Pacific coast and the high plains of Peru. The main features of these predominantly urban cultures are the precocious prominence of metallurgy and the art of making textiles; on the other hand, their architecture lacks the characteristic South American complexity and majesty and there was no system of writing and apparently no method of recording time.

For these reasons it is difficult to reconstruct the sequence of development in this civilisation; in fact the dates that can be inferred from the successive layers of archaeological discoveries and from the most recent radiocarbon research (which has only been carried out sporadically), have not yet made it possible to establish any reliable chronology. The end of these cultures as indigenous entities is usually fixed in 1532, with the arrival of the Spanish conquerors, while their beginning is tentatively dated at about 1000 BC, while 3000 BC is generally taken as the starting date of an agricultural community on the northern coast of Peru, before the era of ceramics. (The oldest Peruvian ceramic known is dated between 1225-850 BC.) One of the chronological classifications applied for convenience by students to the civilisation of the Central Andes allows for the existence of three different successive periods: a Formative period, a classical, 'Full Flowering' or 'Master Craftsmen' period, and a post-classical period. The Chavín style, one of the first to appear according to the latest radiocarbon dating, probably began after 900 BC at the latest and was also found outside its principal seat—the important ceremonial centre of Chavín de Huantar at Cupisnique, in the valley of Chicama, Ancón and Supe on the northern and central coast. It is not known if there were any political links between these various centres; it is certain however that there was a strong religious link (it is possible to distinguish near the communal dwellings large and imposing buildings dedicated to the same cult) and the stylised feline motif characteristic of Chavín work is found everywhere from the central coast to the region of the high northern plains. The most commonly found example of earthenware is a cup with a flat base in black, brown or red, with simple geometrical incisions. The large quantities of ceramics from the cemeteries of Cupisnique are more complex from a pictorial point of view: pitchers with a massive stirrup-type spout, among which are some in the form of humans, animals or vegetables and others of spherical shape with incisions to mark tusks and eyes. In the Casma valley, at Cerro Sechín, the earthenware seems to be of Chavín type but the decorative motifs are different, which suggests that the work may belong to a slightly different period. The second phase of the Formative Period (which is also described as the Late Formative Period because of the many important innovations in all fields of technique) involves the entire coastal region as well as a few places on the high plateaux, and its duration is still controversial; some date it from the 1st century AD, others from the 2nd.

As far as the coastal region is concerned, the valley

of Virú provides a complete and documented archaeological sequence as a result of the excavations carried
out immediately after the second World War. Even
domestic earthenware shows evidence of the im-
proved composition of the impasto, which is finer and
of a more uniform grain because of more careful firing.
Such cultures as those of Salinar, Paracas, Chanapata,
Gallinazo or Virú belong to this period. The first of
these is notable chiefly for the discoveries made in the
ancient cemeteries in the valley of Chicama; the
earthenware, which is of the 'white on red' type, is
decorated in the prevailing manner (which contrasts
with the earlier monochrome ceramics) including a
variety of forms, some of them elaborate, including
the stirrup-type mouthpiece (a common feature),
elongated necks and handles with straps. In other
spherical receptacles the spout is set diagonally and is
linked by a flat, bridge-type handle to a carved figure.
Human and animal figures are also often found
nestling on the top of the vessels and, at Cupisnique,
are depicted more or less realistically. Characteristic
of this style are the vessels in the shape of houses and
temples, represented with interesting and individual
details. Negative painting, which perhaps derived
from the high northern Andean plateaux and in the
Chicama coastal region dates from about 500 BC, appears in the Gallinazo culture but developed further
during the classical period, as can be seen from its
presence in the Paracas culture. This culture was subdivided by Julio C. Tello, who conducted excavations

56. Vessel in human shape. Height 11 in. Paracas Cavernas, Paracas peninsula, Peru. Nationalmuseet, Copenhagen.

56.   Vessel in human shape. Height 11 in. Paracas Cavernas, Paracas peninsula, Peru. Nationalmuseet, Copenhagen. Paras ceramics are produced by a variety of techniques: the application of separately made carved sections; two-colour negative painting; polychrome painting after firing; and the use of incision on the decorative borders.

57.   Vessel representing a deer with its young. Height $10\frac{1}{2}$ in. Northern coast of Peru. British Museum, London. The rich variety of Mochica vessels includes many unusual examples. In this sensitive portrait, the animal is portrayed in a human pose.

58.   Globular vessel with stirrup handle and painting of a warrior. Height $11\frac{1}{2}$ in. Northern coast of Peru. Museo Nacional de Antropología y Arqueología, Lima. Scenes of war are a favourite subject in Mochica painted earthenware. The human and divine figures are painted with an extraordinary lightness of touch in a beautiful shade of red on a cream-coloured background.

59.   Vessel in the shape of a human head with stirrup handle. Height 11 in. Northern coast of Peru. Museo Nacional de Antropología y Arqueología, Lima. These receptacles, also described as portrait-vessels, provide an extraordinary gallery of different physical types, represented in a more-or-less realistic style. The strong modelling and accurate colouring are evidence of an art that had reached full maturity.

60.   Rectangular vessel surmounted with an animal figure holding a human head between its front claws. Height $6\frac{1}{2}$ in. Northern coast of Peru. Museo de América, Madrid. A complex and energetically modelled vessel whose decoration, predominantly creamy-white and red, has a meticulous, almost precious, quality.

57. Vessel representing a deer with its young. Height 10½ in. Northern coast of Peru. British Museum, London.

58. Globular vessel with stirrup handle and painting of a warrior. Height 11½ in..Northern coast of Peru. Museo Nacional de Antropología y Arqueología, Lima.

59. Vessel in the shape of a human head with stirrup handle. Height 11 in. Northern coast of Peru. Museo Nacional de Antropología y Arqueología, Lima.

60. Rectangular vessel surmounted with an animal figure holding a human head between its front claws. Height 6½ in Northern coast of Peru. Museo de América, Madrid.

in this arid peninsula in 1925, into Paracas Cavernas and Paracas Necropolis—names derived from the two different types of burial. In the first, burial chambers were dug deep in the rocky earth; near these were found several mummified bodies covered with fabric and ceramics of various shapes: simple cups with a very wide mouth in heavy impasto, dishes, vessels with a bridge-type handle and double spout and others in which the mouth is supported by a modelled head, often of feline type; a characteristic feature is the roundness of the base, which is typical of the south coast. The impasto is usually dark in colour—orange or brown—while the geometrical decoration includes applied or modelled parts, or, typically, a two-tone colouring either in negative style or added just after firing, in canary yellow, green, red and black and emphasised by incised borders; there are also some highly stylised human figures painted and incised in the same way. The earthenware of Paracas Necropolis (which is believed to be of later date) is very similar to that just described, although the impasto is lighter and the predominating tones are brown and ivory; no reliable dating has yet been established for this work although one phase seems to have been contemporary with the 2nd century AD. Moreover, the most recent research shows that the culture that flourished in the Nazca valleys must have been in close contact with that of Paracas, whose last stage probably occurred earlier than the initial period known as Nazca A.

The second period, which, as we have seen, is known both as the classical period and that of the Master Craftsmen, saw the maturing of the techniques already described and the strengthening of politically powerful centres, which succeeded in developing cultures with clearly defined individual characteristics, in spite of active exchange between them; these include the Mochica, Recuay, Nazca, Tiahuanaco and Pucara cultures although it is possible to trace the beginnings of some, such as those of Nazca and Tiahuanaco, to the preceding period.

According to the few dates so far discovered by the radiocarbon method, the Mochica culture can be said to have begun approximately about 400 BC, and to have lasted until about the end of the 9th century AD. Initially it was centred in the northern valleys of Chicama, Moche and Virú (in the last of these it was partly contemporary with the Gallinazo culture); it then extended southwards as far as the Casma valley. The consistency and importance of the ruins and works of art show that the Mochica were not only highly developed culturally, but also politically and religiously. Mochica domestic earthenware underwent a great number of changes, although it kept its principal qualities of simplicity and utility. But Mochica art achieved its greatest splendour in the field of ceremonial ceramics. These are principally distinguished by their predominantly sculptural character, skilful modelling and sensitive pictorial decoration. The clay is well-baked and thin, its wide range of

61. Vessel representing a feline animal clawing a man.
Height 4½ in. Upper stretch of the Santa river, Peru.
Musée de l'Homme, Paris.

61. Vessel representing a feline animal clawing a man. Height 4½ in. Upper stretch of the Santa river, Peru. Musée de l'Homme, Paris. In Recuay ceramics, richly fantastic themes are found alongside more simple subjects. The structure of the vessels, like the decoration, is fairly complex, even overloaded, though always characterised by a certain vigour.

62. Vessel representing an animal. Height 7 in. Southern coast of Peru. Museo Nacional de Antropología y Arqueología, Lima. Simple shapes are common in Nazca ceramic art whereas modelling is rare and, as a rule, fairly elementary and not always completely successful. Polychrome colouring, on the other hand, is rich and sophisticated; often as many as ten colours are used in one object.

63. Polychrome drum-shaped vessel. Height 1 ft 5 in. Southern coast of Peru. Museum of Primitive Art, New York. Animal motifs are one of the principal features of Nazca decoration; here, for example, the eyes consist of two fish and there is a snake running down the middle of the body.

64. Vessel with bridge-type spout and carved head. Height 5 in. Southern coast of Peru. Museo Nacional de Antropología y Arqueología, Lima. This kind of mouthpiece is a typical feature of Nazca art. The stylised designs of masks and human heads repeated around the base show that this object belongs to a later period when more realistic representation had been superseded.

62. Vessel representing an animal. Height 7 in. Southern coast of Peru. Museo Nacional de Antropología y Arqueología, Lima.

63. Polychrome drum-shaped vessel. Height 1 ft 5 in. Southern coast of Peru. Museum of Primitive Art, New York.

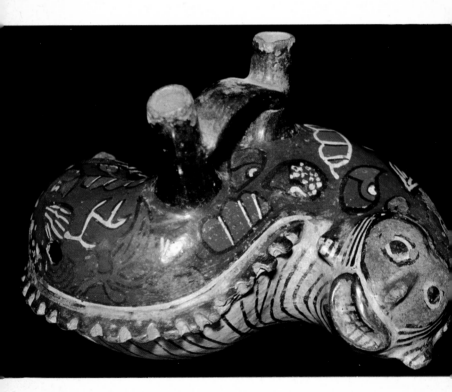

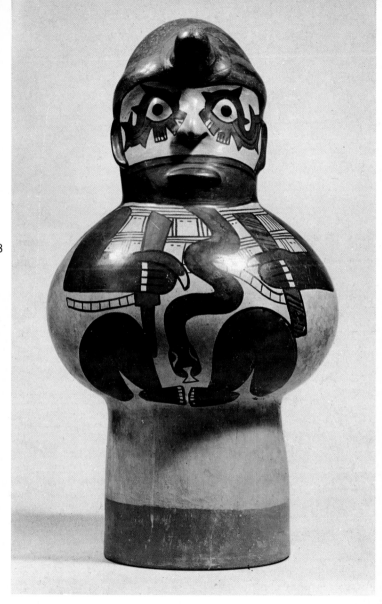

63

64. Vessel with bridge-type spout and carved head. Height 5 in. Southern coast of Peru. Museo Nacional de Antropología y Arqueología, Lima.

colouring produced by variations in oxidation during firing. The forms also differ: the most common is the spout with a stirrup handle, of which the varying forms may reflect different chronological periods. (Larco Hoyle, the well-known expert on Mochica art, uses these differences as a basis for a tentative system of chronology.) Other shapes are globular vessels with a flat base, double vessels, hollow or flattened cups, jars and bottles with necks modelled in various ways; there are many vessels in human, animal or vegetable form, including portrait-vessels, which are often highly realistic. Much of the earthenware is moulded, while the stirrup-type spout and decorative details are added afterwards.

The decoration consists of incisions, reliefs or details pressed on with moulds, sometimes emphasised with colour, while realistic and stylised motifs, in red on buff or white on a red ground, are always painted on a slip. The richness and minute detail of the decoration, which is highly graphic, provide valuable information about this culture. Its flora and fauna are amply illustrated, either in isolation or else as a background to more complex scenes. People are represented in a lively fashion and in great detail as members of social, religious and political hierarchies, as participants in the rituals of life and death, in illness and in the activities of daily life. The same is true of the gods, human, animal or demoniac. From the tombs of Recuay at Callejón de Huavlas in the northern plateaux comes a type of earthenware whose technique and quality seem inferior to Mochica art, although they are its equals in the variety of their shapes, the inventiveness of their subject matter and the richness of their decoration. Although its style is somewhat different, the feline motif appears both as a modelled and a painted decoration: negative painting is widely and elaborately applied in the form of stylised geometrical and zoomorphic motifs, carried out in multiple combinations of white and red.

The Nazca and Ica valleys in the southern coastal regions were the centre of a culture of a greater importance (according to the most recent studies by Duncan Strong) than originally supposed. The remains of the ancient city of Cahuachi, brought to light by Strong in the basin of the Nazca river, are among the earliest in this region. The succeeding period, known as Nazca A, is the most important from the artistic point of view. During the following period, known as Nazca B, the clay, which during Nazca A is thin and well baked, becomes gradually heavier and rougher. The polychrome decoration, which achieves effects as rich as any found on the continent, at first included more realistic subjects, executed on a red and white ground, but gradually evolved towards motifs that are highly stylised and more richly coloured on a predominantly white ground. This development can be attributed to chronological evolution, but also to regional differences, since radiocarbon dating is not yet fully confirmed. The decorative subjects include subjects from nature such

65. Double-bodied vessel. Height 9 in. Northern coast of
Peru. Museo Nacional de Antropología y Arqueología, Lima.

65. Double-bodied vessel. Height 9 in. Northern coast of Peru. Museo Nacional de Antropología y Arqueología, Lima. Here a monkey, depicted with a fair amount of realism and grace, is joined to a highly abstract fruit. Chimú vessels are usually greyish-black, but some examples are a cream and reddish colour.

66. Vessel in the shape of a human head. Height 1 ft 6 in. Northern coast of Peru. Museo Nacional de Antropología y Arqueología, Lima. The stylistic elements here are obviously of Nazca origin and do not derive from the polychrome colour range typical of Tiahuanaca. The great expansion of the Tiahuanaca culture in Peru, particularly during its late period, was the reason for this mixing of influence.

67. Vessel in the shape of a llama. Height 2 ft 3½ in. Southern coast of Peru. Museo Nacional de Antropología y Arqueología, Lima. This animal is frequently represented in Peruvian art, not only in ceramics but also in stone, silver and gold; it is also often used as a motif in textiles. Animal subjects are rare in Tiahuanaca art, which is usually abstract and conventional.

66. Vessel in the shape of a human head. Height 1 ft 6 in.
Northern coast of Peru. Museo Nacional de Antropologia y
Arqueología, Lima.

67. Vessel in the shape of a llama. Height 2 ft 3½ in.
Southern coast of Peru. Museo Nacional de Antropología y
Arqueología, Lima.

as feline animals, fish, birds, fruit, vegetables, religious and mythological themes but more often they consist of human faces with animal and demoniac elements. The human head is a favourite theme and is treated in many different ways; sometimes it is reduced to a stylisation of its various features, which become purely decorative motifs. The most common shapes found are wide-mouthed cups, dishes, chalices, globular forms with two spouts linked by a flat bridge; vessels completely or partly modelled in human and animal shapes are more widespread in the Nazca B style.

On the high plateaux two centres—Pucara in Peru and Tiahuanaco in Bolivia (*c*. 8th—11th century AD) —were outstanding during the classical period, but the second, which developed a few centuries later, not only dominated the culture of its period but succeeded in rapidly extending its influence over the major part of the central Andes, either changing or quite simply submerging the various local styles. The archaeologist Bennett, who conducted a series of excavations in the area between 1932 and 1934, has suggested a sub-division of Tiahuanaco into three stylistic phases: Preclassical, Classical and Decadent. The first phase includes a few examples of pottery in a thick and heavy clay, brown or black, painted in four or five colours; its most typical shape is a small cup that narrows at the neck and widens again at the top. The pottery of the classical period is finer; the colours, which are painted on a base coat of red or light yellow, are brighter, and the ornamentation includes a few geometrical shapes, though the recurrent theme is that of human figures and animals —the puma and the condor (a large vulture)—highly stylised and surrounded with black or white lines. This decoration, always somewhat rigid, is almost reduced to a series of symbols in accordance with the Andean tradition. A typical example is a tall, wide-mouthed beaker, known as a *kero,* and there are also bottles, cups and zoomorphic vessels. The decadent period produced, in addition to less elegant shapes, a type of decoration that was rougher and less precise both in its range of themes and in its colours; the stylisation is even more pronounced and geometrical shapes predominate. At the end of the classical period the Tiahuanaco culture expanded towards the coastal regions of Peru, where it imposed itself on local styles. Although the ceramics produced in this area are notable for their refined polychrome colouring and include shapes similar to those found in Bolivia, their mingling of different stylistic elements reveals the presence of local traditions underlying the borrowings from Tiahuanaco.

The Chimú culture, which developed in the fertile valleys of Lambayeque and Piura, and extended as far south as the Casma valley, may be considered as a second flowering of the Mochica culture, although it was modified by the influence of Tiahuanaco. This period is characterised by the formation of important urban centres, mainly devoted to strategic and

68. Vessel in the shape of a jaguar. Height 10½ in. Central coast, Peru. Museo Nacional de Antropología y Arqueología, Lima.

68.   Vessel in the shape of a jaguar. Height 10½ in. Central coast, Peru. Museo Nacional de Antropología y Arqueología, Lima. This type of vessel is uncommon in Chancay art; the more usual shapes are simple dishes, often with a hollow mouthpiece, and sometimes oval-shaped with facial features depicted on their necks in modest relief. This article was probably influenced by Mochica art.

69.   Vessel in the shape of a hunchback. Height 1 ft 5 in. Santarém, State of Pará, Brazil. University Museum, Philadelphia. Many terracottas, in a variety of fantastic styles, come from a cemetery that probably existed on the site of the present day city of Santarém. This figure, designed in an unusually sober style, carries a bell in his hand and a wallet slung from his shoulder.

70.   Amphora. Height 3 ft 4 in. Cuzco, Peru. University Museum, Philadelphia. An example of Inca ceramic art, which on the whole was poorer than those of earlier cultures from the point of view of human or animal representation and of decoration and colouring. Polychrome colouring appeared only during the late period while the decorative motifs, usually geometric, are repeated somewhat mechanically.

71.   Vessel on a pedestal. Height 10 in. Santarém, State of Pará, Brazil. University Museum, Philadelphia. The most common type of vessel from this culture has a richness of composition and decoration in somewhat unusual taste. The decoration consists of added human and animal heads carved in relief and of incised features and lines.

69. Vessel in the shape of a hunchback. Height 1 ft 5 in.
Santarém, State of Pará, Brazil. University Museum,
Philadelphia.

70. Amphora. Height 3 ft 4 in. Cuzco, Peru. University Museum, Philadelphia.

71. Vessel on a pedestal. Height 10 in. Santarém, State of
Pará, Brazil. University Museum, Philadelphia.

ceremonial purposes; the Chimú centre, the city of Chanchán situated near Trujillo, seems to date from no earlier than the 12th-13th century. From their predecessors, the Chimú adopted only monochrome ceramics—red, yellowish, or of a typical grey-black colour. The shapes of the vessels are varied and unpredictable: the most frequent type is a globular container with a flat base and a stirrup handle. Also found are whistle vases and numerous representations of persons, animals, fruit and vegetables, objects and scenes from daily life, and even mountains. The vessels are usually made with moulds and decorated with sections made in relief or else modelled; painted decoration is rare.

The Chancay ceramics of the central coastal region (which date from shortly before the Inca conquest) unlike the products of the area as a whole, have no particular originality and largely exemplify the stylistic traits of the north and south. The pottery is characterised by an oval-shaped vessel, often large, with a wide neck on which occasionally a human face is modelled, while the limbs are outlined in relief on the body of the vessel itself. The clay is light and porous, pinkish-grey in colour, and the rough surface is often covered with a creamy-white plaster, on which the anatomical features (if any) or stylised or geometrical designs are traced in black or brown.

In the southern coastal region (in the Ica valley and those adjacent to it) a light and well-baked type of ceramic has been found in the form of spherical and oval vessels narrowing at the spout as well as of various types of cups. These are light red or brown in colour, decorated in black, white or red, with geometrical motifs often derived from textiles, or with extremely stylised designs of fish and birds.

During the last period in the history of Precolumbian Peru, the Inca empire, after developing from a more or less insignificant centre, succeeded in less than a hundred years in imposing its religion and its social structure on communities as far north as Ecuador and as far south as Chile. It was not completely broken up until the Spanish conquest of 1532. During this rapid expansion the Inca assimilated the more interesting characteristics of the peoples they had conquered, offering in exchange their own technical and artistic knowledge. The recent excavations carried out by Rowe at Cuzco, the capital city of the Inca dynasty from about 1200, indicate the existence of a primitive period which produced pottery reminiscent, although less refined, of later work. Inca ceramics are easily recognisable; the shapes are few and fairly simple. The most characteristic include the *aryballos* (so-called because it has been inaccurately compared with the Greek vase of this name), which sometimes stands as high as $4\frac{1}{2}$ feet; a shallow cup with a short handle ending in a small human or animal head; a dish with a pedestal and sometimes a cover; also beakers, jars and bottles decorated with simple motifs in red and black on a brown background. It is interesting to note that Inca shapes are found, with slight modifications or in a different clay mixture, in practically all the areas under their domination; one example is the *aryballos* in the typical Chimú blackware. There is however a later type of superior quality characterised by polychrome colouring, known as polychrome Cuzco. The most usual decoration is based on simple, geometrical, but somewhat lifeless, motifs in red, yellow, orange, black and white; there are also examples of stylised representations of butterflies, birds and other creatures.

To conclude this survey of the most important styles that flourished in South America during the Precolumbian era, we should point out the great difference, both geographically and culturally, between the Andean region, densely populated and the seat of large urban societies, and the vast area of the tropical forest to the east of the Andes. Here natural conditions prevented the formation of large organised communities, and although traces of a well-developed aesthetic taste can sometimes be seen in the fragments of local products, it is nevertheless accepted that a larger and more stable society provides a better basis for the rise of a civilisation. Further, there is no evidence that there was any stable tradition in this part of the continent, although at the start of its cultural history it seems to have had a certain influence on Andean art.

LIST OF ILLUSTRATIONS   Page

Height 11 in. Northern coast of Peru. Museo Nacional de Antropología y Arqueología, Lima.